Dinosaurs
and Creatures of the Cretaceous

LEVEL 2 READER

Millions of years ago, dinosaurs ruled the Earth! Some of the best-known dinosaurs appeared starting 150 million years ago, right before and during the Cretaceous (Krih-TAY-shuss) Period. The Cretaceous Period ended 65 million years ago—when dinosaurs suddenly disappeared from the Earth.

Will you ever meet one of these big creatures? No. Most creatures of the Cretaceous died out. But if you look closely at some birds, you may catch a glimpse of a little dino...

Stegosaurus

Pronunciation: steg-oh-SAWR-us
Name means: *Roof lizard*
Family: Stegosauridae
Lived: 150 million years ago
Areas found: USA (Colorado, Utah, Wyoming), Europe
Length: 30 ft (9 m)
Height: 14 ft (4.3 m)
Weight: 2–5 tons
Diet: low plants

Stegosaurus was an herbivore (plant eater). It had a large body with two rows of bony plates along its back. It was slow-moving, but it had tail spikes for weapons. It had a tiny head and small brain.

Archaeopteryx

Pronunciation: AR-kee-OP-ter-ix
Name means: *Ancient wing*
Family: Archaeopterygidae
Lived: 155–150 million years ago
Areas found: Germany
Height: 1 foot (0.3 m)
Length: 3 feet (0.9 m)
Weight: 2 pounds
Diet: insects

Dinosaurs looked like big reptiles, but in many ways they were built like birds. This feathered creature was a cross between a bird and a dinosaur. *Archaeopteryx* ate insects, which it caught in flight.

Brachiosaurus

Pronunciation: BRAK-ee-oh-SAWR-us
Name means: *Arm lizard*
Family: Brachiosauridae
Lived: 153–113 million years ago
Areas found: Algeria, Portugal, Tanzania, USA (Colorado, Utah, Wyoming)
Length: 82 ft (25 m)
Height: 42 ft (12.8 m)
Weight: 45–55 tons
Diet: conifers, cycads, ferns

Brachiosaurus was one of the largest land animals ever to have existed. This plant-eating giant had a long neck to reach treetops. It had a huge body, a long tail for balance, and a tiny brain.

Iguanodon

Pronunciation: ig-WAN-oh-don
Name means: *Iguana tooth*
Family: Iguanodontidae
Lived: 140–110 million years ago
Areas found: Great Britain, Mongolia, USA
Height: 16 feet (4.9 m)
Length: 30–40 feet (9–12 m)
Weight: 3–5 tons
Diet: plants

Iguanodon was the first creature discovered and recorded as a dinosaur. It had a long snout and a toothless beak, used for grazing on low plants. It had a spike on each thumb, used as a weapon.

Utahraptor

Pronunciation: YOO-tah-RAP-tor
Name means: *Utah's predator*
Named by: Kirkland, Gaston & Burge, 1993
Family: Dromaeosauridae
Lived: 132–119 million years ago
Areas found: USA (Utah)
Height: 8 feet (2.4 m)
Length: 22 feet (6.6 m)
Weight: 1500 pounds
Diet: other dinosaurs

Utahraptor was a fierce predator. It may have hunted in packs, bringing down large prey. Each back foot had a curved claw that could grow to 10 inches (25 cm) long! Scientists now believe that *Utahraptor* had feathers—but could not fly.

Baryonyx

Pronunciation: bare-ee-ON-ix
Name means: *Heavy claw*
Family: Baryonychidae
Lived: 120 million years ago
Areas found: Great Britain, Nigeria
Height: 6 feet (1.8 m)
Length: 35 feet (10.7 m)
Weight: 4,400 pounds
Diet: fish, carcasses (dead animals)

The first *Baryonyx* bone was found in England in 1983. It is one of the few known piscivorous (fish-eating) dinosaurs. It had a long snout and narrow jaws, very similar to a crocodile's.

Carnotaurus

Pronunciation: KAHRN-uh-TAWR-us
Name means: *Flesh-eating bull*
Family: Abelisauridae
Lived: 97 million years ago
Areas found: Argentina
Height: 13 feet (4 m)
Length: 25 feet (7.5 m)
Weight: 2,000 pounds
Diet: herbivorous dinosaurs

You would not want to meet this guy during the Cretaceous Period! *Carnotaurus* was a carnivore (meat eater) with a huge mouth and sharp teeth. It had horns and spikes down its back. It probably had tough, pebbly skin like a reptile.

Pteranodon

Pronunciation: ter-ON-oh-don
Name means: *Winged toothless*
Family: Pteranodontidae
Lived: 89–70 million years ago
Areas found: USA
Length: 15–20 feet (4.5–6 m)
Wingspan: 25 feet (7.6 m)
Diet: fish

Pteranodon was not a dinosaur. It was a flying reptile. It had a toothless beak like a modern bird. It could soar through the air on the skin-flaps between its extra-long finger bones and body.

Velociraptor

Pronunciation: veh-LOSS-i-RAP-tor
Name means: *Swift thief*
Family: Dromaeosauridae
Lived: 83–70 million years ago
Areas found: China, Mongolia
Height: 2.5 feet (0.8 m)
Length with tail: 6 feet (1.8 m)
Weight: 33 pounds
Diet: herbivorous dinosaurs

Velociraptor was a quick, smart hunter! It was small—about the size of a turkey—with a long tail for balance. The sharp, curved claw on each foot was a deadly tool. *Velociraptor* probably had feathers, but could not fly.

Hadrosaurus

Pronunciation: HAD-ruh-SAWR-us
Name means: *Bulky (sturdy) lizard*
Lived: 80 million years ago
Areas found: Canada, USA
(Montana, New Jersey, New Mexico, South Dakota)
Height: 15 feet (4.6 m)
Length: 25–33 feet (7.5–10 m)
Weight: 3 tons
Diet: plants

Hadrosaurus is also known as a "duckbilled dinosaur." It had a wide, flat beak for scooping up plants. This was the first dinosaur skeleton ever put together to display.

Parasaurolophus

Pronunciation: par-ah-SAWR-OL-uh-fus
Name means: *Like Saurolophus*
Family: Lambeosauridae
Lived: 76–73 million years ago
Areas found: North America
Height: 16 feet (4.9 m)
Length: 33 feet (10 m)
Weight: 3–4 tons
Diet: plants

This "duckbilled" dinosaur lived in herds. It had a long, hollow crest on top of its head. *Parasaurolophus* may have used this crest to make trumpeting noises to call to other members of the herd.

Troödon

Pronunciation: TROH-uh-don
Name means: *Wounding (gnawing) tooth*
Family: Troödontidae
Lived: 76–70 million years ago
Areas found: USA, Canada
Height: 3 feet (0.9 m)
Length: 6.5–10 feet (2–3 m)
Weight: 110 pounds
Diet: small mammals, reptiles

Troödon may have been one of the smartest dinosaurs. It had large eyes and hands that could hold onto prey. Some *Troödon* egg nests have been found—but the eggs have fossilized and turned to stone.

Chasmosaurus

Pronunciation: KAZ-muh-SAWR-us
Name means: *Cleft lizard*
Family: Ceratopsidae
Lived: 76–70 million years ago
Areas found: Canada
Height: 8 feet (2.4 m)
Length: 17 feet (5.2 m)
Weight: 3,000 pounds
Diet: plants

Chasmosaurus had a small nose horn and two long brow horns. It had a large frill that covered the back of its neck. This wide frill may have frightened predators away.

Styracosaurus

Pronunciation: stih-RAK-uh-SAWR-us
Name means: *Spiked lizard*
Family: Ceratopsidae
Lived: 75–72 million years ago
Areas found: Canada, USA (Montana)
Height: 9 feet (2.7 m)
Length: 18 feet (5.5 m)
Weight: 3 tons
Diet: fibrous plants

Look at that nose horn! And the spikes on that neck frill! Yikes! Predators had to be careful around *Styracosaurus*. These dinosaurs may have been herd animals, traveling in large groups.

Edmontonia

Pronunciation: ED-mon-TON-ee-a
Name means: *From Edmonton*
Family: Nodosauridae
Lived: 76–68 million years ago
Areas found: USA
Height: 6 feet (1.8 m)
Length: 23 feet (7 m)
Weight: 3.5 tons
Diet: low-lying plants

Edmontonia was built like a tank. It had thick skin and bony plates, like armor. Those spikes kept predators away. This gentle "tank" only ate plants.

Corythosaurus

Pronunciation: ko-RITH-uh-SAWR-us
Name means: *Helmet lizard*
Family: Lambeosauridae
Lived: 75 million years ago
Areas found: Canada, USA
Height: 21 feet 6.4 m)
Length: 33 feet (10 m)
Weight: 4.2 tons
Diet: plants

Corythosaurus had a bony crest on its head. The cassowary birds that live today in Australia have a similar crest. Perhaps these creatures are distant cousins!

Gallimimus

Pronunciation: gal-ih-MY-mus
Name means: *Chicken mimic*
Family: Ornithomimidae
Lived: 73–65 million years ago
Areas found: Mongolia
Height: 11 feet (3.4 m)
Length: 20 feet (6 m)
Weight: 1000 pounds
Diet: small vertebrates, insects, plants

Gallimimus looked more like a large bird than a reptile. It had a long neck and toothless beak, similar to the ostrich of Africa and the emu of Australia.

Torosaurus

Pronunciation: TOR-oh-SAWR-us
Name means: *Protuberance (or pierced) lizard*
Family: Ceratopsidae
Lived: 70–65 million years ago
Areas found: USA, Canada
Height: 8 feet (2.4 m)
Length: 23 feet (7 m)
Weight: 5–7 tons
Diet: plants

Torosaurus had one of the largest skulls of any known land animal—almost 9 feet! Its nose horn and huge brow horns would scare any predator! It may have been the last of the horned dinosaurs.

Archelon

Pronunciation: AR-chi-lone
Name means: *Ancient turtle*
Family: Protostegidae
Lived: 70 million years ago
Areas found: USA (South Dakota, Kansas, Nebraska)
Length: 13.5 feet (4 m)
Width: 16 feet (4.9 m)
Weight: 5,000 pounds
Diet: mollusks, squid

Archelon was a Cretaceous creature, but not a dinosaur. It was the largest sea turtle that has ever lived—as big as a car! And it probably had a lifespan of more than 100 years.

Ankylosaurus

Pronunciation: ang-KIE-lo-SAWR-us
Name means: *Stiffened lizard*
Family: Ankylosauridae
Lived: 68–65 million years ago
Areas found: Western North America
Length: 20–33 ft (6–10 m)
Height: 5.5–9 ft (1.7–2.7 m)
Weight: 3–4 tons
Diet: ferns, mosses,
low-lying plants

Ankylosaurus had its own bony armor to protect it from carnivores. It also had a big clubbed tail that could injure a predator's face or legs. Stand back!

Triceratops

Pronunciation: try-SAIR-a-tops
Name means: *Three-horned face*
Family: Ceratopsidae
Lived: 68–65 million years ago
Areas found: Canada, USA (Montana, North Dakota, South Dakota, Wyoming)
Length: 26–30 ft (8–9 m)
Height: 9.5 ft (2.9 m)
Weight: 6–10 tons
Diet: fibrous plants

Triceratops is one of the best-known dinosaurs. Its sharp brow horns were useful weapons. It ate only plants with its parrot-like beak, and grew to be as big as an elephant.

Tyrannosaurus Rex

Pronunciation: ter-RON-o-sawr-us REX
Name means: *Tyrant lizard king*
Family: Tyrannosauridae
Lived: 68–65 million years ago
Areas found: Asia, Canada,
USA (Colorado, Montana, New Mexico, Wyoming)
Length: 43 ft (13 m)
Height: 20 ft (6 m)
Weight: 6–7.5 tons
Diet: herbivorous dinosaurs,
carcasses

The Cretaceous "king" was *Tyrannosaurus Rex*
—one of the largest meat-eating animals to ever
live! It looks fierce, but it fed mainly on
dead animals.